Learn Svelte

A. De Quattro

Copyright © 2024

Guide to Svelte

1.Introduction to Svelte

Svelte: the revolutionary web development framework

In an increasingly wide landscape of frameworks and libraries for web development, Svelte stands out for its innovative approach and superior performance. Introduced in 2016 by Rich Harris, creator of Rollup, Svelte quickly gained popularity among developers for its simplicity, lightweight nature, and effectiveness in generating optimized and high-performing code.

But what makes Svelte so different from other frameworks like React, Angular, or Vue? The answer lies in how Svelte handles component rendering and application state management. While most frameworks rely on a virtual DOM-based approach and reconciliation, Svelte takes a completely different approach.

In Svelte, components are written using a templating language similar to HTML, enriched with reactive features and special directives. When compiled, Svelte code is transformed into pure JavaScript code, without the use of a virtual DOM. This approach enables the generation of lighter and faster code, eliminating the need to perform costly reconciliation operations.

Additionally, Svelte adopts a declarative programming model, making it easy to write clear and readable code, facilitating the maintenance and scalability of applications. Thanks to its intuitive syntax and rich documentation, developers can quickly learn how to use Svelte and deepen their knowledge.

Another key aspect of Svelte is its native integration with code optimization techniques, such as tree-shaking and the generation of minified and performance-optimized code. This means that Svelte applications can be faster and lighter than counterparts based on other frameworks, ensuring a superior user experience.

Finally, Svelte is supported by a vibrant community of developers and enthusiasts who actively contribute to its development and dissemination. Through forums, tutorials, online courses, and conferences, it is possible to deepen one's knowledge of Svelte and share experiences with other community members.

In conclusion, Svelte emerges as a revolutionary web development framework that offers superior performance, lightweight code, intuitive syntax, and an active and collaborative community. If you are looking for an innovative way to develop fast and efficient web applications, Svelte could be the right choice for you.

2. Installation of Svelte

Svelte is a modern and versatile framework for developing web applications, which sets itself apart from traditional frameworks like React, Angular, and Vue due to its approach to compiling components directly in JavaScript code, rather than using a virtual DOM. This allows for better performance and reduces the browser's workload during element rendering.

Installing Svelte is quite simple and can be done by following a few key steps. Initially, it is necessary to ensure that Node.js is installed on your system. Node.js is a JavaScript-based runtime environment that allows for running JavaScript code outside the browser. It is available for different platforms, including Windows, macOS, and Linux.

Once Node.js installation is confirmed, you can proceed with installing Svelte using the npm package manager, which is automatically installed with Node.js. To begin, you will need to create a new project folder and open the terminal in the newly created directory. Subsequently, you can run the following command to create a new Svelte project using the official template:

```
npx degit sveltejs/template my-svelte-project
```

This command will copy all the necessary files to start developing with Svelte into the `my-svelte-project` folder. Once the operation is complete, you can navigate to the project directory and install the necessary dependencies by running the command:

```
cd my-svelte-project
npm install
```

At this point, the Svelte project has been successfully installed and configured on your system. To start a local development server and view the application in a browser, you can run the command:

```
npm run dev
```

This command will start a local server at `http://localhost:5000`, allowing you to view and test the application in real-time. During development, you can modify the Svelte files in the `src` folder and save changes to see them reflected immediately in the browser.

Once the development of the Svelte application is complete, you can create an optimized build for release by running the command:

```
npm run build
```

This command will generate an optimized version of the application ready to be published on a web server or in a production environment. The build will be saved in the `public` folder.

In conclusion, the installation of Svelte is a simple process that requires a few steps and can be done quickly using npm. Svelte provides a fast and efficient development experience, thanks to its ability to compile components directly in JavaScript code and ensure optimal performance during application execution. With Svelte, you can easily and intuitively create modern and high-performance web applications.

3. How to get started with Svelte Basic concepts of Svelte Components and Properties and Constraints

Svelte is a front-end framework known for its ease of use, lightweightness, and optimal performance. In this article, I will guide you through the basic concepts of Svelte, components and properties, as well as the constraints you need to know to start using it.

To begin, it is important to understand the concept of "components" in Svelte. Components are reusable blocks of code that contain logic, styles, and HTML markup, which can be used multiple times within a web application. Components in Svelte are separate files with the extension ".svelte" and usually represent specific portions of a web page, such as a navigation bar, a contact form, or an image gallery.

To create a new component in Svelte, you need to create a new file with the extension ".svelte" and define the HTML markup, CSS styles, and JavaScript logic within it. For example, if you want to create a button component, the code could look like this:

```html
<script>
  // Define JavaScript logic
</script>

<button style="background-color: blue; color: white; padding: 10px;">Click here</button>
```

Once you have created the component, you can use it within another web page by including it with the `<ComponentName />` tag. For example:

```html
<main>
  <h1>Welcome to Svelte!</h1>
  <ComponentName />
</main>
```

In addition to components, another fundamental concept in Svelte is "properties". Properties are values that can be passed from a parent component to a child component to customize the behavior and appearance of the child component. Properties in Svelte are declared inside the angle brackets `<>` of the child component tag and can be accessed using the `export` keyword.

For example, if you want to pass a "text" property to the button component we defined earlier, the code could look like this:

```html
<script>
  export let text = "Click here";
</script>

<button style="background-color: blue; color: white; padding: 10px;">{text}</button>
```

To use the component with the defined properties, you can do so as follows:

```html
<main>
  <h1>Welcome to Svelte!</h1>
  <ComponentName text="Click here to get started" />
</main>
```

Finally, it is important to understand constraints in Svelte. Constraints are rules that you can define to control and limit the data within your web application. For example, if you want the text of the button we defined earlier to always be in uppercase, you can use a constraint like this:

```html
<script>
  export let text = "Click here";
</script>

<button style="background-color: blue; color: white; padding: 10px;">{text.toUpperCase()}</button>
```

Constraints allow you to maintain data consistency within your application and ensure that certain rules are adhered to.

In conclusion, Svelte is a front-end framework that offers a new perspective on web application development. With the basic concepts of Svelte, such as components, properties, and constraints, you can efficiently and effectively create performant and scalable web applications.

4. Svelte Event Directives

Event directives are a way to handle user interactions such as clicks, hover, or keyboard input within our web applications. In Svelte, event directives are handled very efficiently and intuitively, making programming user interactions much simpler and more readable.

Event directives in Svelte are similar to those available in other frameworks like React or Vue, but with some significant differences that make them particularly powerful. One key feature of event directives in Svelte is the ability to add more than one event handler to a single HTML element, greatly simplifying the management of complex interactions.

Another interesting feature of event directives in Svelte is the ability to pass parameters to the events themselves. For example, you can pass specific data or variables from the application to the event handling function, allowing further customization of the user interaction behavior.

Additionally, event directives in Svelte are tightly integrated with the framework's reactivity system, allowing events to interact seamlessly with the application state and respond dynamically to its changes. This enables the creation of dynamic and responsive user interfaces without having to write complex state update logic.

One of the most commonly used events in Svelte is definitely the click event. With the {on:click} directive, you can assign an event handling function to an HTML element that will be executed every time the user clicks on it. This is particularly useful for handling actions such as opening a dropdown menu, submitting a form, or navigating to another page.

Another common event is hover, used to handle user interactions when the cursor hovers over a specific element. With the {on:hover} directive, you can perform actions like showing a tooltip, changing the style of the element, or starting an animation when the user hovers over it.

Event directives in Svelte can also be used to handle keyboard-related events, such as key presses. With the {on:key} directive, you can assign handling functions to key press events, allowing you to create more interactive and accessible user interfaces.

Thanks to the simplicity and power of event directives in Svelte, it is possible to efficiently and intuitively handle user interactions within our web applications. In addition to basic directives like click, hover, and keyboard input, Svelte also offers the ability to create custom directives to manage more complex and specific interactions.

Event directives in Svelte are a fundamental tool for creating dynamic and responsive user interfaces, greatly simplifying the management of user interactions within our web applications. With their simplicity and power, Svelte event directives are a valuable ally for developers looking to create engaging and intuitive user experiences.

To use a directive in Svelte, it is enough to add the corresponding attribute to the desired HTML element. For example, to create an element that hides and shows with a click, we can use the `on:click` directive. Here is an example of how this code might look like:

```html
<script>
 let isVisible = false;

 function toggleVisibility() {
   isVisible = !isVisible;
 }
</script>

<button on:click={toggleVisibility}>
 Toggle visibility
</button>

{#if isVisible}
 <div>
   This is visible text
 </div>
{/if}
```

In this example, we have defined a variable `isVisible` and a function `toggleVisibility()`. When the user clicks the button, the `toggleVisibility()` function is called and changes the state of the `isVisible` variable. The `on:click` directive associates the click event of the button with the `toggleVisibility()` function.

Svelte directives can be customized with modifiers that allow adding additional functionality. For example, we can use the `preventDefault` modifier to prevent the default behavior of an HTML element within a directive. Here is an example of how this code might look like:

```html
<a href="https://www.google.com" on:click|preventDefault>
 Click here to visit Google
</a>
```

In this case, the `preventDefault` modifier prevents the link from navigating to the destination page when the user clicks on it. This is particularly useful when you want to perform a custom action without the page being reloaded.

Svelte directives offer many advanced features that allow creating complex and dynamic user interfaces easily and quickly. For example, you can use the `bind` directive to directly bind the input values of HTML elements to variables in the component. Here is an example of how this code might look like:

```html
<script>
 let inputValue = '';
</script>

<input type="text" bind:value={inputValue} placeholder="Enter some text">
<p>The input value is: {inputValue}</p>
```

In this example, the `bind:value` directive binds the input element's value to the `inputValue` variable. When the user enters text in the input, the variable's value is automatically updated and displayed on the page.

Another useful directive is `on:input`, which allows running code every time the user enters text in an input element. For example, you can use this directive to check the length of the entered text and display an error message if it exceeds a certain length. Here is an example of how this code might look like:

```html
<script>
 let inputValue = '';

 function handleInput(event) {
   inputValue = event.target.value;

   if (inputValue.length > 10) {
     alert('Maximum allowed length is 10 characters');
   }
 }
</script>

<input type="text" on:input={handleInput} placeholder="Enter some text">
```

In this example, the `handleInput()` function is called every time the user enters text in the input. The length of the entered text is checked, and if it exceeds 10 characters, an error message is displayed.

Svelte directives allow creating responsive and dynamic user interfaces easily and efficiently. By using custom directives and modifiers, you can add advanced features to components and enhance the user experience. Svelte is a powerful framework that offers many customization possibilities and flexibility, making it an ideal choice for developing modern and high-performance web applications.

5. State Management with Svelte Reactive Variables Local and Global State Management Using store for Managing Shared State

One of the key features of Svelte is state management through reactive variables, which allow tracking of changes in the code and automatically updating the user interface accordingly.

Reactive variables in Svelte are declared using the '$:' prefix before the variable itself. For example, if we want to create a reactive variable called 'count' we can do so as follows:

```
let count = 0;
$: doubleCount = count * 2;
```

In this case, whenever the value of the 'count' variable changes, the 'doubleCount' variable will be automatically computed accordingly. This makes state management in the application very simple and intuitive.

Additionally, Svelte offers the ability to

manage state both locally and globally. To manage state locally within a component, we can simply declare variables within the script of the component itself. For example, if we want to create a local state for a counter within a component, we can do so as follows:

```
<script>
  let count = 0;
</script>

<button on:click={() => count += 1}>Increment</button>
<p>{count}</p>
```

In this case, whenever the 'Increment' button is clicked, the counter will be incremented by one and the user interface will be automatically updated to reflect the new value of the counter.

To manage state globally within a Svelte application, we can use the store. The store in Svelte is an object that allows sharing state between different components of the application in a simple and safe manner. To create a store, we can use the 'writable' function of Svelte as follows:

```
import { writable } from 'svelte/store';

export const count = writable(0);
```

Once the store is created, we can use it within our components to access and modify its state. For example, if we want to create two components that share the same state of a counter, we can do so as follows:

Component 1:

```
<script>
  import { count } from './store.js';
</script>

<button on:click={() => count.update(n => n + 1)}>Increment</button>
<p>{$count}</p>
```

Component 2:

```
<script>
  import { count } from './store.js';
```

```
</script>

<p>{$count}</p>
```

In this case, both components will use the same 'count' store to keep track of the counter state. When one of the components modifies the counter state, the other component will be automatically updated to reflect the change.

Svelte offers a simple and intuitive way to manage state within applications through the use of reactive variables, local state, and the store for managing shared state. These features make Svelte an ideal choice for developing reactive and performance-driven user interfaces.

6. Routing in Svelte Configuration of routes Navigation between pages Passing parameters between pages

Routing in Svelte is a fundamental concept for creating efficient and well-structured web applications. Thanks to the routing system, routes can be defined within the application, which are the paths that the user can follow to navigate between different pages and sections of the site. In this way, content can be organized clearly and intuitively, facilitating navigation and improving the user experience.

The configuration of routes in Svelte is done through the use of a dedicated module called 'svelte-routing'. This module provides functionalities for defining routes and managing navigation within the application. To start using the routing system in Svelte, it is necessary to install the 'svelte-routing' module using a package manager like npm or yarn:

```bash
npm install svelte-routing
```

Once the module is installed, it can be used

within Svelte components to define routes and manage navigation between pages. To begin, import the necessary components from the 'svelte-routing' module in the main project file:

```javascript
import { Router, Route } from 'svelte-routing';
```

Subsequently, different routes can be defined within the Router component, specifying the route path and the component to display when that route is reached. For example, to define three main routes within the application, we can write:

```html
<Router>
   <Route path="/" component={Home} />
   <Route path="/about" component={About} />
   <Route path="/contact" component={Contact} />
</Router>
```

In this way, we have defined three main routes: the main route ("/") that displays the Home component, the "/about" route that displays the About component, and the "/contact" route that displays the Contact component. When the user navigates within the application and reaches one of these routes, the respective component will be displayed on the page.

To facilitate navigation between pages, links can be added within Svelte components using the Link component provided by 'svelte-routing'. This component allows creating links that redirect the user to the specified route when clicked. For example, to create a link to the "/about" route, we can write:

```html
<Link to="/about">About</Link>
```

In this way, when the user clicks on the "About" link, they will be redirected to the "/about" route and will see the About component displayed on the page.

Another important feature of the routing system in Svelte is passing parameters between different pages. This allows making the content displayed within components dynamic based on data passed as parameters through the URL. For example, if we want to pass a dynamic parameter to the "/user" route to display the profile of a specific user, we can define the route as follows:

```html
<Route path="/user/:id" component={User}/>
```

In this case, the parameter ':id' represents a dynamic parameter that can be different for each user. To retrieve the parameter passed within the User component, the 'params' parameter provided by the Route component can be used:

```javascript
<script>
   export let params;
</script>
```

This way, the 'id' parameter can be accessed within the User component using 'params.id' and the information related to the specified user can be displayed.

The routing system in Svelte allows for efficiently organizing and structuring web applications, facilitating user navigation between different pages and sections of the site. Thanks to route configuration, easy navigation, and passing of parameters between pages, engaging and personalized user experiences can be created, thereby improving the quality and usability of the application.

7. Animations in Svelte Using Transitions Creating Custom Animations Managing Animation Events

Animations in Svelte are a fantastic way to make your web projects dynamic and engaging. Thanks to its intuitive syntax and efficient state management capabilities, Svelte allows you to create smooth and engaging animations with minimal effort. In this article, we will explore how to use Svelte's built-in transitions, create custom animations, and manage animation events.

Using Transitions in Svelte

Svelte provides a set of built-in transitions that you can use to add animation effects to your components. To use a built-in transition in Svelte, you simply add it as an attribute to your HTML element. For example, to add a fade-in effect to an element, you can use the `fade` transition.

Here's an example of using the `fade` transition in Svelte:

```html
<script>
```

```
  import { fade } from 'svelte/transition';
</script>

<style>
  div {
    transition: opacity 0.3s;
  }
</style>

<div transition:fade>
  This text is fading in.
</div>
```

In the example above, we imported the `fade` transition from the `svelte/transition` module and applied it to the `<div>` element. The `fade` transition will handle the opacity change of the element during the animation.

Creating Custom Animations in Svelte

If Svelte's built-in transitions don't meet your needs, you can easily create custom animations using the `<svelte:transition>` and `<svelte:await>` tags.

To create a custom transition in Svelte, you need to define two functions: `leave` and `intro`. The `leave` function handles the element's animation when it is removed from the DOM, while the `intro` function handles the element's animation when it is inserted into the DOM.

Here's an example of creating a custom slide-in transition in Svelte:

```html
<script>
   function slide(node, { delay = 0 }) {
      return {
         delay,
         duration: 500,
         css: t => `transform: translateX(${t * 100}%)`,
      };
   }
</script>

<style>
   div {
      transition: transform 0.5s;
   }
</style>

<div in:slide={{delay: 100}}>
   This text is sliding in.
</div>
```

In the example above, we defined the `slide` function that handles the slide-in animation for the `<div>` element. The function takes two arguments: `node`, which represents the element itself, and an optional `{ delay }` object representing any delay in executing the animation. The function returns an object with properties `delay`, `duration`, and `css`, which are used to define the animation.

Managing Animation Events in Svelte

To manage animation events in Svelte, you can use the `on:` modifier to listen for various events of the animating element. For example, you can use `on:animationstart`, `on:animationend`, and `on:animationcancel` to respectively handle the start, end, and cancellation of an animation.

Here's an example of handling the `animationend` event in Svelte:

```html
<script>
   let isAnimating = false;

   function handleAnimationEnd() {
      isAnimating = false;
   }
```

```
</script>

<style>
  div {
    transition: transform 0.5s;
  }
</style>

<div
  on:animationend={handleAnimationEnd}
  class:animate={{isAnimating}}
>
  This text is animated.
</div>
```

In the example above, we defined a `isAnimating` variable that tracks the animation state. When the animation ends, the `animationend` event triggers the `handleAnimationEnd` function which sets the `isAnimating` variable to `false`, indicating that the animation has ended.

Svelte provides excellent support for creating and managing animations, making it easy to add dynamic visual effects to your web projects. By using Svelte's built-in transitions, creating custom animations, and managing animation events, you can make your web interfaces more engaging and interactive.

8.Optimizing performance with Svelte Lazy loading of resources

One of the most effective ways to improve a website's performance is to implement lazy loading of resources, which means loading resources only when they are actually needed.

In this article, we will focus on performance optimization using Svelte, a reactive JavaScript framework that emphasizes simplicity and performance. We will see how to implement lazy loading of resources in a Svelte application to improve loading speed and reduce resource consumption.

What is lazy loading of resources?

Lazy loading of resources is a performance optimization technique that involves loading a website's or a web application's resources only when they are actually needed. This means that images, scripts, and other elements of the site are loaded only when the user needs them, thereby reducing loading time and resource consumption.

Implementing lazy loading of resources with Svelte

To implement lazy loading of resources in a Svelte application, we can leverage JavaScript's dynamic importing feature. This feature allows us to dynamically load a module only when it is called in the code, rather than loading it immediately when the application starts.

Here is an example of how to implement lazy loading of resources in a Svelte application:

```javascript
<script>
  let lazyLoadedModule;

  const loadModule = async () => {
    if (!lazyLoadedModule) {
      // Dynamically load the module only when needed
      lazyLoadedModule = await import('./LazyLoadedModule.svelte');
    }
  };
</script>

<button on:click={loadModule}>Load module</button>

{#if lazyLoadedModule}
```

```
  <svelte:component this={lazyLoadedModule.default} />
{/if}
```

In this example, we have created a `loadModule` function that dynamically loads the `LazyLoadedModule.svelte` module only when the "Load module" button is clicked. Once the module is loaded, we display it using the special `svelte:component` directive.

Benefits of lazy loading of resources in Svelte

Implementing lazy loading of resources in a Svelte application brings several benefits in terms of performance and user experience:

1. Reduced loading time: By loading resources only when needed, the Svelte application will be lighter and faster to load for users.

2. Resource savings: By loading only the necessary resources, browser resource consumption is reduced, and bandwidth waste is avoided.

3. Improved user experience: Users will see an improvement in the application's performance,

with faster loading times and increased responsiveness.

Lazy loading is a technique used to defer the loading of non-essential resources at the initial page load, thereby optimizing performance by reducing the amount of content that needs to be loaded upfront. This can be particularly beneficial for websites that have a lot of images, videos, or other large assets that may not be immediately visible to the user.

In this example, we will demonstrate how to implement lazy loading of resources in a Svelte application to improve performance.

Let's say we have a website with a gallery of 100 images that are displayed in a grid. Instead of loading all 100 images at once, we can lazily load them as the user scrolls down the page.

First, we will create a Svelte component called `LazyImage.svelte` that will render an image tag with a lazy loading attribute:

```html
<script>
  import { onMount } from 'svelte';
```

```
  let src = '';
  let loaded = false;

  const lazyLoad = () => {
    const observer = new IntersectionObserver((entries, observer) => {
      entries.forEach(entry => {
        if (entry.isIntersecting) {
          src = entry.target.dataset.src;
          observer.unobserve(entry.target);
          loaded = true;
        }
      });
    });

    observer.observe($$('img'));
  };

  onMount(() => {
    lazyLoad();
  });
</script>

{#if loaded}
  <img {src} alt="Lazy loaded image"/>
{:else}
  <img src="#" alt="Placeholder image"/>
{/if}
```

In this component, we are using the `IntersectionObserver` API to detect when the image comes into view. When the image is intersecting the viewport, we set the `src` attribute of the image tag to the value of the `data-src` attribute, which will be the actual image URL. We also set a `loaded` flag to control when the image is actually loaded.

Next, we will update our main component to render a list of `LazyImage` components, each with a different `data-src` attribute representing the image URL:

```html
<script>
   import LazyImage from './LazyImage.svelte';

   let images = Array.from({ length: 100 }, (_, index) => ({
      url: `https://example.com/image-${index + 1}.jpg`
    }));
</script>

{#each images as { url }, index}
   <LazyImage data-src={url} key={index}/>
{/each}
```

Now, when the main component is rendered, it will lazily load each image as the user scrolls down the page, resulting in improved performance by reducing the initial load time and bandwidth usage.

In conclusion, lazy loading resources in a Svelte application can significantly improve performance by deferring the loading of non-essential content until it is actually needed. By implementing lazy loading techniques, we can create a more responsive and efficient user experience while also optimizing the use of network resources.

In conclusion, implementing lazy loading of resources in a Svelte application is an effective way to optimize performance and improve the user experience. By using JavaScript's dynamic importing feature, you can load resources only when they are actually needed, thereby reducing loading time and browser resource consumption. If you are looking to improve your web application's performance, consider using lazy loading of resources in combination with Svelte to achieve impressive results.

9. Bundle splitting CSS Removal with Svelte

One of these practices is removing unused CSS, which can be unnecessary weight for the page.

One way to do this is bundle splitting, a technique that involves splitting JavaScript and CSS into different bundles so that they are only loaded when needed. In this article, we will explore how to implement bundle splitting for removing unused CSS with Svelte, a reactive JavaScript framework.

What is Svelte?

Svelte is a JavaScript framework that allows developers to create reactive and performant user interfaces. Unlike other frameworks like React or Angular, Svelte moves the framework logic from the browser to compile time. This means that Svelte code is translated to native JavaScript during the compilation process, eliminating the need for additional libraries during code execution.

Why remove unused CSS

Unused CSS can significantly slow down the loading of web pages. When a browser downloads CSS that is not actually used, it is essentially wasting resources processing that file. This can greatly slow down page loading and overall user experience.

Removing unused CSS can lead to faster loading times, a better user experience, and a reduction in the amount of data the browser has to download. This is particularly important for websites with many pages or that load on mobile devices with slower internet connections.

How to implement bundle splitting with Svelte

To implement bundle splitting with Svelte and remove unused CSS, you need to follow some steps:

1. Use Svelte with rollup: Rollup is a module bundler for JavaScript that is often used with Svelte to bundle code optimized for performance. Make sure to set up your Svelte project to use Rollup as the bundler.

2. Use dynamic imports: Dynamic imports are an ES6 feature that allows you to import

modules asynchronously during code execution. By using dynamic imports, you can load CSS files only when needed, instead of loading them all at once.

3. Separate CSS into separate files: To enable CSS bundle splitting, it is important to separate CSS into separate files and dynamically import these files within Svelte code. This way, CSS will only be loaded when needed, improving the overall site performance.

4. Use inline classes and styles: To further reduce the weight of CSS and improve performance, you can use inline classes and styles directly in the HTML code instead of defining everything in the CSS file. This will further reduce the number of file requests and make the site more responsive.

Bundle splitting is a powerful technique for optimizing website performance and removing unused CSS. By using Svelte with Rollup and dynamic imports, you can easily implement bundle splitting and significantly improve site performance. Removing unused CSS can lead to faster loading times, a better user experience, and an overall more responsive website. If you are a developer looking for ways to optimize your website's performance, consider implementing bundle splitting with Svelte to remove unused CSS.

10.Testing with Svelte Using Jest for unit tests

Jest is a popular testing framework for JavaScript that provides a comprehensive testing experience with a powerful set of features. It is widely used for unit testing in JavaScript projects and can be easily integrated with Svelte to test components.

To start testing Svelte components with Jest, you need to install Jest and the related support packages. Here is a brief guide on how to configure Jest for testing Svelte components:

1. Install Jest and related packages:
```
npm install --save-dev jest @testing-library/svelte @testing-library/jest-dom svelte-jester
```

2. Create a Jest configuration file (jest.config.js) and specify the following parameters:
```javascript
module.exports = {
  preset: 'jest-preset-svelte',
  moduleFileExtensions: ['js', 'svelte'],
```

```
  transform: {
    '^.+\\.js$': 'babel-jest',
    '^.+\\.svelte$': 'svelte-jester'
  },
  setupFilesAfterEnv: ['@testing-library/jest-dom/extend-expect']
}
```

3. Create a sample test for a Svelte component:
```javascript
// Counter.test.js

import { render, fireEvent } from '@testing-library/svelte';
import Counter from '../Counter.svelte';

test('renders counter component', () => {
  const { getByText } = render(Counter);

  expect(getByText('Count: 0')).toBeInTheDocument();
});

test('increments count when button is clicked', () => {
  const { getByText } = render(Counter);
  const button = getByText('Increment');
```

```
  fireEvent.click(button);

  expect(getByText('Count: 1')).toBeInTheDocument();
});
```

4. Run the tests with Jest:

```
npx jest
```

This is just an example of how you can test Svelte components using Jest. You can extend these tests by adding tests for other use cases and components in your application.

Examples of tests for Svelte components

Now that you are familiar with Jest and how to test Svelte components, let's explore some examples of tests for different types of Svelte components. We will see how to test simple components, components using props, and components with events and state.

1. Testing a simple component:

A simple component can be tested by verifying that the component is rendered correctly and that a specific element is present in the DOM.

```javascript
// SimpleComponent.test.js

import { render } from '@testing-library/svelte';
import SimpleComponent from '../SimpleComponent.svelte';

test('renders simple component', () => {
  const { getByText } = render(SimpleComponent, { props: { text: 'Hello world' } });

  expect(getByText('Hello world')).toBeInTheDocument();
});
```

2. Testing a component with props:

If a component uses props to customize its behavior, you can test that the component behaves correctly with different values for the props.

```javascript
// PropsComponent.test.js
```

```javascript
import { render } from '@testing-library/svelte';
import PropsComponent from '../PropsComponent.svelte';

test('renders props component', () => {
  const { getByText } = render(PropsComponent, { props: { title: 'Test Title', description: 'Lorem ipsum' } });

  expect(getByText('Test Title')).toBeInTheDocument();
  expect(getByText('Lorem ipsum')).toBeInTheDocument();
});
```

3. Test di un componente con eventi e state:

Se un componente gestisce eventi e stato internamente, è possibile testare che il componente si comporti correttamente quando si verificano determinati eventi o quando lo stato cambia.

```javascript
// StateComponent.test.js

import { render, fireEvent } from '@testing-
```

```
library/svelte';
import StateComponent from '../StateComponent.svelte';

test('increments count when button is clicked', () => {
  const { getByText } = render(StateComponent);
  const button = getByText('Increment');

  fireEvent.click(button);

  expect(getByText('Count: 1')).toBeInTheDocument();
});
```

End-to-end testing with Cypress with Svelte

In addition to unit tests, it is important to also test the overall functionality of the application with end-to-end tests. Cypress is a popular end-to-end testing tool that allows you to write tests with a simple and intuitive syntax.

To start using Cypress with Svelte, you need to install Cypress and its supporting packages. Here is a brief guide on how to set up Cypress to test a Svelte application:

1. Install Cypress and related packages:

```
npm install --save-dev cypress @cypress/svelte
```

2. Initialize the Cypress project:

```
npx cypress open
```

3. Create an example end-to-end test for a Svelte application:

```javascript
// app.spec.js

describe('App', () => {
  it('should display welcome message', () => {
    cy.visit('http://localhost:5000');

    cy.contains('Welcome to Svelte App').should('be.visible');
  });
});
```

4. Run the tests with Cypress:

```
npx cypress run
```

This is just an example of how you can test a Svelte application with Cypress. You can expand these tests by adding tests for other features and scenarios of the application.

Conclusion

Testing Svelte components is essential to ensure that the application is robust and error-resistant. By using Jest for unit tests and Cypress for end-to-end tests, you can thoroughly test Svelte components and ensure code quality.

Throughout this article, we have explored how to test Svelte components with Jest and Cypress and provided examples of tests for different types of Svelte components. By following testing best practices and writing thorough tests for Svelte components, you can develop robust and high-quality web applications.

11. Deployment of a Svelte Build application

Deployment of an application is a crucial phase in the development of a software project, which involves making the application available to end users. In this article, we will focus on the deployment of a Svelte Build application, which is a web application developed with the Svelte framework.

Svelte is a modern framework for creating web user interfaces, which differentiates itself from other frameworks like React and Angular by its build-time compilation approach. This means that Svelte converts the source code into optimized JavaScript code during the build process, rather than converting the code during application execution like other frameworks do. This approach leads to optimized performance and a better user experience.

Before proceeding with the deployment of the Svelte Build application, it is important to ensure that the development steps have been completed and the application has been built. To create the Svelte application Build, simply use the `npm run build` command in the terminal, which will generate the optimized files ready for deployment.

Once the build files are obtained, you can proceed with the deployment of the application. There are several ways to deploy a Svelte Build application, depending on the user's needs and preferences. Below, we will analyze the main deployment methods of a Svelte Build application.

1. Deployment on a web server
One of the most common methods for deploying a Svelte Build application is to deploy it on a web server. To do this, you need access to a web server on which to upload the build files. This server can be either a physical server or a cloud server, such as Amazon Web Services or Google Cloud Platform.

To deploy the Svelte Build application on a web server, you can use a file transfer protocol like FTP or SFTP. Simply upload the build files to the web server's web directory and the application will be available online.

2. Deployment on a hosting service
An alternative solution to deploying on a web server is to deploy on a dedicated hosting

service. There are numerous hosting services that offer the ability to easily deploy a web application without the need to manage a web server.

There are hosting services specifically for Svelte applications, such as Firebase Hosting or Vercel, that simplify the deployment of a Svelte Build application. Simply upload the build files to the hosting service and the application will be immediately available online.

3. Deployment on a CDN
A third method of deploying a Svelte Build application is to deploy it on a Content Delivery Network (CDN). CDNs are network services that efficiently distribute web content, reducing application loading times.

To deploy the Svelte Build application on a CDN, you can use a CDN service like Cloudflare or Amazon CloudFront. Simply upload the build files to the CDN service and configure web traffic routing to the Svelte application.

Regardless of the chosen deployment method, it is important to keep in mind some best practices to optimize the deployment process and ensure optimal performance of the Svelte Build application.

Before deploying the application, it is good practice to perform comprehensive testing of the application to verify proper operation and resolve any bugs or issues. Additionally, it is advisable to configure environment variables correctly and securely manage access keys and sensitive data.

In conclusion, the deployment of a Svelte Build application is a fundamental process in the distribution of a software project and requires attention and care to ensure optimal performance and correct usability by end users. With the right practices and tools, it is possible to achieve effective and efficient deployment, making the Svelte Build application available securely and reliably.

Deployment of a Svelte application: Build of the application with examples

The deployment of a web application is a crucial step in making your project available to end users. In this article, we will focus on the deployment of a Svelte application, a modern JavaScript framework for creating responsive and performant user interfaces.

The deployment process of a Svelte application involves creating an optimized bundle of the application, which will then be uploaded to a server to be made accessible to users through a web browser. This article will step by step guide you on how to build a Svelte application and how to distribute it online.

Prerequisiti

Prima di iniziare il deployment dell'applicazione Svelte, è necessario aver già sviluppato l'applicazione e averla testata localmente. Assicurati di avere Node.js e npm installati nel tuo sistema, in quanto sono necessari per eseguire i comandi di build e deployment.

Step 1: Create a new Svelte project

If you haven't created a Svelte project yet, you can do so by running the following command in the terminal:

```
npx degit sveltejs/template my-svelte-project
```

This command will download the base template of a Svelte project into the "my-svelte-project" folder. Enter the project folder with the following command:

```
cd my-svelte-project
```

Step 2: Install project dependencies

Once inside the project folder, run the following command to install project dependencies:

```
npm install
```

This command will install all the necessary libraries and packages for the Svelte application to function.

Step 3: Build the application

To create an optimized bundle of the Svelte application, you can run the following command:

```
npm run build
```

This command will compile all the JavaScript, CSS, and HTML files of the application into a single bundle optimized for production. Once the build process is complete, the application bundle will be located inside the "public" folder.

Step 4: Deploy the application to a server

To deploy the Svelte application to a web server, you can use various options such as Netlify, Vercel, GitHub Pages, AWS, and many more. In this article, we will use Netlify as an example hosting platform.

Netlify

1. Open your browser and go to [Netlify](https://www.netlify.com/).
2. Click on "Sign up" to create a free account on Netlify.
3. Once registered, click on "New site from Git" and select the repository of the Svelte project.
4. Configure the project settings (such as the branch to use and the build command) and click on "Deploy".
5. Netlify will start the build and deployment

process of the Svelte application. Once completed, the application will be available online at the address generated by Netlify.

In conclusion, in this article we have seen how to deploy a Svelte application, starting from creating a new Svelte project to distributing the application on a web server. By using the commands and hosting platforms outlined in this article, you will be able to easily make your Svelte project available to users worldwide. Happy deployment!

Code Example

```javascript
<script>
  let count = 0;

  function increment() {
    count += 1;
  }

  function decrement() {
    count -= 1;
  }
</script>

<main>
  <h1>Counter: {count}</h1>
```

```
  <button on:click={increment}>Increment</button>
  <button on:click={decrement}>Decrement</button>
</main>

<style>
  main {
    text-align: center;
    margin-top: 20px;
  }

  button {
    font-size: 1.5rem;
    margin: 0 10px;
    padding: 5px 10px;
    border: 1px solid #333;
    border-radius: 4px;
    background-color: #f0f0f0;
    cursor: pointer;
  }
</style>
```

This is a simple example of a Svelte application that implements a counter. The application keeps track of how many times the user presses an "Increment" or "Decrement" button and displays the result to the user through a reactive and intuitive interface. By using the concepts and techniques illustrated in this example, you will be able to easily create complex and performant Svelte applications to deploy online.

12. Configuration of a Production Server Optimizations for Fast Page Loading with Svelte

The speed of loading web pages is crucial to ensure a good user experience and improve search engine rankings such as Google. To achieve optimal performance, it is essential to properly configure the production server and apply specific optimizations to reduce page loading times.

In this article, we will explore how to configure a production server for a Svelte application and discuss some strategies to optimize page loading and improve overall site performance.

Configuration of the production server

Before starting with specific optimizations for Svelte, it is important to configure the production server properly to ensure efficient deployment of the application. Here are some fundamental steps to follow:

1. Use a high-performance hosting server: choosing a reliable and high-performance hosting provider is essential to ensure optimal

site performance. Make sure to opt for a server with sufficient hardware resources to handle the application workload.

2. Configure the web server properly: correctly setting up the web server is crucial to ensure efficient deployment of the application. Be sure to configure the server parameters properly to optimize performance and ensure secure application deployment.

3. Optimize static resources: use compression and caching techniques to optimize the loading of static resources (such as CSS files, JavaScript, and images) and reduce page loading times.

4. Use a CDN: using a Content Delivery Network (CDN) can help improve site performance by distributing static resources to servers distributed worldwide, reducing latency and improving page loading times.

Optimizations for fast page loading with Svelte

Once the production server is properly configured, you can apply some specific optimizations to improve page loading and optimize Svelte application performance. Here are some strategies to follow:

1. Use code bundling and minimization: use tools like Rollup or Webpack for bundling and minimizing the JavaScript and CSS code of the application. This will reduce file sizes and improve page loading times.

2. Use prerendering: use prerendering to generate static versions of the application pages during the build process. This will improve page loading times and enhance search engine rankings.

3. Optimize images: reduce the size and quality of images used in the application to decrease page loading times. Use image optimization tools like ImageOptim or TinyPNG to reduce file sizes without compromising visual quality.

4. Use lazy loading: implement lazy loading to load images and other non-essential content only when they are viewed by the user. This technique will improve page loading times and optimize application performance.

5. Use prefetching: use prefetching to load necessary resources for upcoming pages in advance, improving navigation smoothness

and reducing loading times for subsequent pages.

Conclusion

Properly configuring a production server and applying specific optimizations to improve page loading are essential steps to ensure optimal performance of a Svelte application. By following the strategies outlined in this article, you can improve page loading times and enhance the user experience.

Always remember to regularly test application performance and monitor page loading times to identify areas for improvement and further optimize site performance. With a correct configuration of the production server and implementation of recommended optimizations, you can ensure fast page loading and a better user experience for site visitors.

13. API Management in Svelte

APIs allow developers to access resources and functionalities external to their website or application, enabling them to integrate third-party services and enhance the user experience.

In Svelte, we can use external APIs to integrate data and functionalities from third parties into our applications.

To get started, it is important to understand the concept of APIs and how we can use them in Svelte. An API (Application Programming Interface) is a set of rules and protocols that allow two applications to communicate with each other. External APIs enable developers to access services and resources offered by third parties, such as data, functionalities, and cloud services.

To manage external APIs in Svelte, we can use the fetch() function, which allows us to make HTTP requests and retrieve data from a remote server. With fetch(), we can fetch information from an external API and use it within our application. For example, we can retrieve data from a geolocation service to display the user's location on a map or get information from a weather service to show the current weather.

Here is an example of how we can use fetch() to retrieve data from an external API in Svelte:

```javascript
<script>
  let data = [];

  fetch('https://api.example.com/data')
    .then(response => response.json())
    .then(json => {
      data = json;
    });
</script>

{#each data as item}
  <p>{item.name}</p>
{/each}
```

In the example above, we are making a GET request to an external API at the URL https://api.example.com/data. Once we receive the response, we convert the data to JSON format and assign it to the data variable. Finally, we use an each block to iterate over the data and display it within our application.

In addition to fetch(), we can also use HTTP request handling libraries such as Axios or the fetch-mock library to simulate HTTP requests during the development and testing of our applications. These libraries allow us to more efficiently handle calls to external APIs and separate the communication logic from the rest of the application.

Another important consideration in managing external APIs in Svelte is error handling. When making a call to an external API, it is important to handle potential exceptions and errors that may occur during the process. We can use the try...catch block to catch errors and handle them appropriately within our application.

Here is an example of how we can handle errors during a call to an external API in Svelte:

```javascript
<script>
  let data = [];
  let error = null;

  try {
    fetch('https://api.example.com/data')
```

```
      .then(response => response.json())
      .then(json => {
        data = json;
      });
  } catch (e) {
    error = e;
  }
</script>

{#if error}
  <p>{error.message}</p>
{/if}
```

In the example above, we are catching any errors generated during the call to the external API and displaying an error message within the application. Properly handling errors is crucial to ensure that the application is robust and responsive to any communication issues with external APIs.

Finally, another aspect to consider in managing external APIs in Svelte is data caching. When retrieving data from an external API, we can store the results of the calls to avoid making the same request again in the future. We can use Svelte's reactive variables to store data in cache and update it only when necessary.

Here is an example of how we can cache data obtained from an external API in Svelte:

```javascript
<script>
  import { onMount } from 'svelte';

  let data = [];
  let cachedData = localStorage.getItem('cachedData');

  onMount(() => {
    if (!cachedData) {
      fetch('https://api.example.com/data')
        .then(response => response.json())
        .then(json => {
          data = json;
          localStorage.setItem('cachedData', JSON.stringify(data));
        });
    } else {
      data = JSON.parse(cachedData);
    }
  });
</script>

{#each data as item}
  <p>{item.name}</p>
{/each}
```

```

In the example above, we are checking if there is cached data in the browser's localStorage. If there is no data in the cache, we make a call to the external API and store the results in the cache for faster future access. Otherwise, we use the data already present in the cache without making new calls to the external API. In conclusion, managing external APIs in Svelte is a fundamental aspect in the development of modern web applications. By using fetch(), libraries for HTTP requests, error handling, and caching storage, we can efficiently and responsively integrate third-party data and functionality into our applications. By experimenting with different techniques and strategies for managing external APIs, we can enhance the user experience and make our applications more performant and reliable.
```

14. Example of creating an application with Svelte

In this article, I will guide you step by step in creating a sample application using Svelte. We will start from installing the necessary tools to building a small application that you can explore and modify to your liking.

Before we begin, make sure you have Node.js installed on your system. If you haven't already, you can download it from the official website and follow the installation instructions.

Step 1: Creating a new Svelte project

To get started, open the terminal and create a new folder for your project. Navigate into this folder and run the following command to create a new Svelte project:

```
npx degit sveltejs/template svelte-app
```

This command creates a new folder called `svelte-app` with the basic structure of a Svelte project. Enter the newly created folder with the command `cd svelte-app` and install the project dependencies by running `npm install`.

Step 2: Displaying a welcome text

Once the dependencies are installed, open the file `src/App.svelte` with your favorite text editor. This is where we will write the code to display a simple welcome text.

Replace the content of the file with the following code:

```html
<script>
  let name = 'world';
</script>

<main>
  <h1>Hello {name}!</h1>
  <p>Welcome to this sample application built with Svelte.</p>
</main>

<style>
  main {
    text-align: center;
    margin: 2rem;
  }
```

```
  h1 {
    color: #333;
  }
</style>
```

This code defines a variable `name` with the default value `"world"` and displays a title and a welcome paragraph inside a `main` element. Feel free to modify the text and style to your liking.

Step 3: Running the application and viewing it in the browser

Once you have finished editing the `App.svelte` file, you can start the integrated development server of Svelte by running the command `npm run dev` from the root of your project. This command will start a local server and automatically open your browser to the address `http://localhost:5000`.

When you view the application in the browser, you should see the welcome text that you defined in the `App.svelte` file. If you modify the text and save the file, the web page will automatically update to reflect your changes thanks to the reactivity of Svelte.

Step 4: Implementing a counter feature

Now that you have completed the introduction phase, let's move on to implementing a counter feature that allows you to increment a value with a button.

Once again, modify the `App.svelte` file by adding the following code inside the `<script>` tag:

```html
<script>
  let count = 0;

  function increment() {
    count += 1;
  }
</script>
```

Then, add the following code after the welcome paragraph to display the value of the counter and a button to increment the value:

```html
<p>Counter: {count}</p>
<button on:click={increment}>Increment</button>
```

```

Inside the `<script>` tag, we defined a variable `count` initialized to 0 and a `increment` function that increments the value of `count` by 1 on each button click. In the HTML, we added a paragraph to display the counter value and a button that calls the `increment` function on click.

Save the file and see how your application now displays a counter that you can increment by clicking the button.

Step 5: Styling the page with CSS

To complete the sample application, let's add some CSS styling to make our page more visually appealing. Modify the `<style>` tag in the `App.svelte` file with the following code:

```css
main {
  text-align: center;
  margin: 2rem;
}

h1 {
  color: #333;
}

```css
p {
  color: #666;
}

button {
  padding: 0.5rem 1rem;
  margin-top: 1rem;
  background-color: #007bff;
  color: white;
  border: none;
  border-radius: 5px;
  cursor: pointer;
}

button:hover {
  background-color: #0056b3;
}
```

```
<script>
  let count = 0;

  function increment() {
    count += 1;
  }

  function decrement() {
    count -= 1;
```

```
  }
</script>

<h1>Counter: {count}</h1>
<button
on:click={increment}>Increment</button>
<button
on:click={decrement}>Decrement</button>

<style>
 h1 {
   font-size: 2em;
   color: #333;
 }

 button {
   padding: 10px 20px;
   margin: 10px;
   font-size: 1em;
   background: #007bff;
   color: #fff;
   border: none;
   cursor: pointer;
 }
</style>
```

This code adds a style to our page, defining colors, margins, padding, and borders for the HTML elements we have defined in our `App.svelte` file. You can experiment with colors and CSS properties to further customize the appearance of your application.

Step 6: Publishing the Application

Once the sample application is completed, you are ready to publish it online to show it to friends and colleagues. To do this, run the command `npm run build` from the root of your project to generate the static files of the application.

When the command is completed, you will have a `public` folder inside your project folder with all the necessary files to publish the application. You can upload this folder to any static hosting service like Netlify or Vercel to make it accessible online.

Conclusion

In this article, we have step by step created a sample application using Svelte, a modern and lightweight front-end framework that is gaining popularity in the web developer community.

We started by creating a new Svelte project and implementing a counter functionality with a button to increase the value. Then, we added CSS styles to enhance the look of the page and finally published the application online to share it with the world.

Svelte offers a different approach to creating responsive and performant user interfaces, eliminating the need for a virtual DOM and making the code simpler and easier to manage. If you are interested in exploring more about this framework, I recommend checking out the official documentation and the many tutorials available online.

15. Implementation of the main features in Svelte

In recent years, Svelte has gained significant popularity among web developers thanks to its simplicity and power. This front-end framework stands out from others as it does not require a library bundle to function, but compiles the code directly into lightweight and performant JavaScript. In this article, we will explore the main features of Svelte and how to implement them in our projects.

1. Components

One of the most powerful aspects of Svelte is its components. With Svelte, we can create reusable components that contain HTML, CSS, and JavaScript in a single file. This allows for greater modularity and ease of code maintenance. To create a component in Svelte, we can define a .svelte file and insert our code inside it. For example, if we wanted to create a button component, the Button.svelte file could look like this:

```
<script>
  let text = "Click here";
```

```
</script>

<style>
  button {
    background-color: #007bff;
    color: white;
    padding: 8px 16px;
    border: none;
    border-radius: 4px;
  }
</style>

<button>{text}</button>
```

This way, we can define the behavior, style, and markup of the button within a single file, making the code more readable and maintainable.

2. Binding

Svelte offers various features to dynamically update the DOM based on changes in data. One of these is binding, which allows us to connect data to HTML elements so that they are automatically updated. For example, if we wanted to create an input field that updates its value in real-time based on a variable, we could do it like this:

```
<script>
  let name = '';
</script>

<input type="text" bind:value={name}>
<p>Hello, {name}!</p>
```

In this way, the value of the input field will always be synchronized with the `name` variable, and every time the field value changes, the greeting string will also be updated.

3. Events

Svelte offers a simple and intuitive system for handling events in a component. We can listen to events such as click, input, submit, and many others directly within the .svelte file. For example, if we wanted to add a click event to our button and change its text on click, we could do it like this:

```
<script>
  let text = "Click here";
```

```
  function changeText() {
    text = "You clicked!";
  }
</script>

<button on:click={changeText}>{text}</button>
```

This way, every time we click the button, the text will change from "Click here" to "You clicked!".

4. Directives

Svelte offers several directives that allow us to manipulate the DOM in a simple and clean way. One of these is the `if` directive, which allows us to conditionally display an element based on the value of a variable. For example, if we wanted to show an element only if a variable is true, we could do it like this:

```
<script>
  let visible = true;
</script>

{#if visible}
  <p>The element is visible</p>
```

```
{/if}
```

This way, the paragraph will be shown only if the `visible` variable is true.

5. Store

Svelte offers a store system that allows us to manage the global state of the application in a simple and efficient way. Stores are observable objects that can be shared among the various components of the application. An example of using stores could be a counter that is shared between two components. To create a store, we can do it like this:

```
import { writable } from 'svelte/store';

export const counter = writable(0);
```

Once the store is created, we can access it in different components and modify it asynchronously. For example, to increment the counter by one in a button, we could do it like this:

```
```

```
<script>
  import { counter } from './store.js';

  function incrementCounter() {
    $counter += 1;
  }
</script>

<button on:click={incrementCounter}>Increment</button>
```

This way, we have access to the `counter` store in different components and can modify it reactively.

In conclusion, Svelte offers an innovative and powerful approach to developing reactive user interfaces. Thanks to its simplicity and advanced features, Svelte is gaining more and more popularity among web developers. With the main features of Svelte described in this article, you can improve the productivity and quality of your front-end code. If you haven't already, I recommend taking a look at this framework and experimenting with its capabilities.

16. Basic Syntax in Svelte

Svelte has a very lightweight and intuitive syntax compared to other frameworks like React or Angular.

In this article, we will explore the syntax of Svelte and see how it can be used to create modern and performant web applications.

Components in Svelte

One of the fundamental concepts of Svelte is that of components, which are modular and reusable units of code that represent specific parts of a web application's user interface. In Svelte, defining a component is extremely simple: just create a file with a .svelte extension and declare a block of HTML code inside it.

For example, suppose we want to create a component that displays a list of items. We can define it as follows:

```html
<!-- List.svelte -->
<script>
  let items = ['Item 1', 'Item 2', 'Item 3'];
```

```
</script>

<ul>
  {#each items as item}
    <li>{item}</li>
  {/each}
</ul>
```

In this example, we are creating a List component that contains a list of items stored in the items variable. Through the {#each} directive, we can iterate over each item in the list and display it inside an <li> tag. This is just a simple example to illustrate the basic syntax of a component in Svelte.

Reactivity in Svelte

Another essential feature of Svelte is reactivity, which allows user interface elements to automatically respond to changes in the application's state. In Svelte, reactivity is handled through the use of reactive variables, which are defined within the <script> section of a component and can be updated to trigger the rendering of elements linked to them.

For example, suppose we want to create a

component that displays a counter and allows the user to increment its value with a button. We can define it as follows:

```html
<!-- Counter.svelte -->
<script>
  let count = 0;

  function increment() {
    count += 1;
  }
</script>

<button on:click={increment}>
  Clicked {count} times
</button>
```

In this example, we are creating a Counter component that contains a count variable initialized to 0. Inside the increment() function, we increment the value of count by 1 every time the user clicks the button. Thanks to Svelte's reactivity, the <button> element is automatically updated with the new value of count whenever it is changed.

Events and Properties

Svelte provides a simple and intuitive way to handle events and properties within components. Events can be defined using the on: directive followed by the event name, while properties can be assigned directly to HTML elements within the component.

For example, suppose we want to create a component that displays an image and allows the user to modify its width and height through two input fields. We can define it as follows:

```html
<!-- Image.svelte -->
<script>
  let width = 200;
  let height = 200;
</script>

<img src="image.jpg" width={width} height={height}>
<input type="range" min="0" max="500" bind:value={width}>
<input type="range" min="0" max="500" bind:value={height}>
```

In this example, we are creating an Image component that displays an image with width and height initialized to 200. Through two range input types, the user can dynamically modify the width and height values, which are immediately reflected in the image thanks to the reactivity of Svelte.

Directives and Conditional Logic

Svelte provides various directives and constructs that allow for easy management of conditional logic and DOM manipulation within components. Some of the most common directives include if, each, and await, which allow for showing or hiding elements based on certain conditions, iterating over arrays of elements, and awaiting the completion of an asynchronous promise.

For example, suppose we want to create a component that displays a different message based on the current time. We can define it as follows:

```html
<!-- Greeting.svelte -->
<script>
  let now = new Date();
</script>
```

```
{#if now.getHours() < 12}
  <p>Good morning!</p>
{:else if now.getHours() < 18}
  <p>Good afternoon!</p>
{:else}
  <p>Good evening!</p>
{/if}
```

In this example, we are creating a Greeting component that displays a different greeting message based on the current time. Thanks to the if directive, we can check the value returned by the getHours() method of the Date object and display the appropriate message to the user.

Conclusions

In this article, we have explored the syntax of Svelte and seen how it can be used to create reactive and performant components within web applications. Svelte offers a simple and intuitive approach to building user interfaces, allowing developers to focus on application logic without worrying about complex frameworks and libraries.

If you are interested in learning more about

Svelte and getting started with it for your projects, we recommend checking out the official documentation at svelte.dev and trying to create some sample components to get familiar with the syntax and features offered by this modern front-end framework.

17. Styles in Svelte

Svelte is a JavaScript framework that is gaining popularity due to its simplicity and lightweight nature. One of the most interesting aspects of Svelte is its ability to separate HTML, CSS, and JavaScript code into three different sections, making the code cleaner and easier to manage. In this article, we will explore some of the styles that can be used in Svelte to create dynamic and engaging user interfaces.

One of the key considerations when working with styles in Svelte is managing inline CSS. Svelte allows you to write CSS directly in the components, eliminating the need to create separate CSS files. This approach simplifies style management and keeps all the code related to a component within it.

To add styles to a Svelte component, you can use the `<style>` tag directly in the component file. For example, if we want to apply a color and font size style to the text inside a component, we can write the following code:

```html
<script>
```

```
  let color = 'red';
  let fontSize = '16px';
</script>

<style>
  p {
    color: {color};
    font-size: {fontSize};
  }
</style>

<p>This is an example of text with dynamic styles in Svelte</p>
```

In this example, we defined two variables `color` and `fontSize` within the `<script>` tag, which are then used in the `<style>` tag to define the text color and size. By using curly braces `{}` you can interpolate the variables directly within the CSS code, making the values dynamic and responsive to changes.

In addition to defining individual styles within a component, you can also use CSS classes to apply styles to multiple elements. To do this, you can define a class within the `<style>` tag and then apply it to one or more HTML elements within the component. For example, if we want to define a class for a gray background and bold text, we can write the following code:

```html
<script>
  let isGrayBackground = true;
</script>

<style>
  .grayBackground {
    background-color: gray;
    font-weight: bold;
  }
</style>

<div class:grayBackground>This is an example of text with gray background and bold font</div>
```

In this example, we defined a class called `grayBackground` that defines a gray background and bold text. We then applied this class to the `<div>` using the syntax `class:className`, where `className` is the name of the class defined within the `<style>` tag.

Una delle caratteristiche più potenti di Svelte è la capacità di utilizzare stili condizionali per applicare stili a elementi in base a determinate condizioni. Ad esempio, se vogliamo modificare lo stile di un elemento in base a una variabile booleana, possiamo farlo facilmente utilizzando la direttiva `{:class}`. Ecco un esempio:

```html
<script>
  let isBold = true;
</script>

<div {:class={bold: isBold}}>This text will be bold if isBold is true</div>
```

In this example, we have defined a variable `isBold` that determines whether the text should be in bold or not. By using the directive `{:class={bold: isBold}}`, we are applying the `bold` class to the `<div>` element only if the `isBold` variable is true.

Another interesting feature that Svelte offers is the ability to use global styles within a component. If there are styles that need to be applied to all components within an application, they can be defined in the `App.svelte` file and imported into individual components. This allows for maintaining style consistency throughout the application without repeating the same CSS code in every component. Here is an example of how to import a global style within a component:

```html
<!-- App.svelte -->
<style>
  body {
    font-family: Arial, sans-serif;
  }

  main {
    padding: 20px;
  }
</style>
```

```

```html
<!-- Component.svelte -->
<style>
 h1 {
   color: blue;
 }
</style>

<h1>This is an example of using global styles in Svelte</h1>
```
```

In this example, we have defined a style for the `body` and the `main` container in the `App.svelte` file, and a style for the `h1` header in the `Component.svelte` file. It is important to note that the styles defined in the `App.svelte` file will be applied globally to all components within the application.

Lastly, another interesting feature of Svelte is the ability to use global variables to define styles that can be shared across multiple components. This is particularly useful when trying to maintain style consistency throughout the application and simplifying the management of colors, sizes, and other common styles. Here is an example of how to use global variables to define shared styles:

```html
<!-- App.svelte -->
<style>
  :root {
    --primaryColor: blue;
    --secondaryColor: red;
  }
</style>
```

```html
<!-- Component.svelte -->
```

```
<style>
  p {
    color: var(--primaryColor);
  }

  button {
    background-color: var(--secondaryColor);
  }
</style>

<p>This text will be in the primary color defined in the global variables</p>
<button>This button will have the secondary color defined in the global variables</button>
```

In this example, we have defined two global variables `--primaryColor` and `--secondaryColor` in the `:root` selector in the `App.svelte` file, and then used them within the `Component.svelte` component to change the text color of the paragraph and the background color of the button. By using global variables to define shared styles, it is easy to change the variable values in one place and have the styles updated in all components that use them.

Svelte offers many interesting features for managing styles within a web application. By utilizing the techniques described in this article, it is possible to create dynamic and visually appealing user interfaces with clean and easy-to-manage styles.

Index

1. Introduction to Svelte pg.4

2. Installation of Svelte pg.7

3. How to get started with Svelte Basic concepts of Svelte Components and Properties and Constraints pg.10

4. Svelte Event Directives pg.14

5. State Management with Svelte Reactive Variables Local and Global State Management Using store for Managing Shared State pg.22

6. Routing in Svelte Configuration of routes Navigation between pages Passing parameters between pages pg.26

7. Animations in Svelte Using Transitions Creating Custom Animations Managing Animation Events pg.31

8. Optimizing performance with Svelte Lazy loading of resources pg.37

9. Bundle splitting CSS Removal with Svelte

pg.44

10.Testing with Svelte Using Jest for unit tests pg.48

11.Deployment of a Svelte Build application pg.56

12.Configuration of a Production Server Optimizations for Fast Page Loading with Svelte pg.66

13.API Management in Svelte pg.70

14. Example of creating an application with Svelte pg.76

15.Implementation of the main features in Svelte pg.85

16.Basic Syntax in Svelte pg.92

17.Styles in Svelte pg.99

www.ingramcontent.com/pod-product-compliance
Lightning Source LLC
Chambersburg PA
CBHW050318230526
45471CB00005B/2250